CONTEN[...]

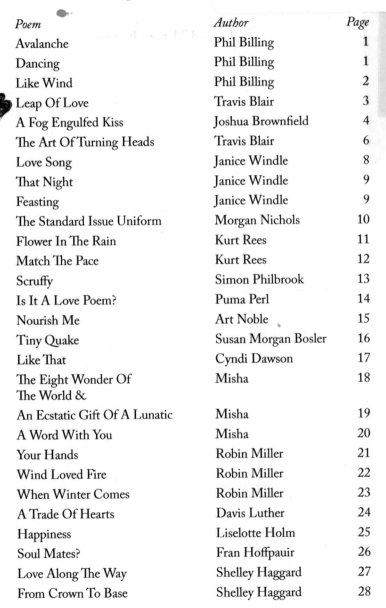

AVALANCHE
Phil Billing.

You come upon me
Like an avalanche
And I am swept away
In the blizzard white
Of a starry night.

I sugar roll
And planet swirl,
I float,
I fly,
And shiver whirl.

I dissolve,
I spin,
And waking find
My lips
Against
Your skin.

DANCING
Phil Billing.

In the garden of my dreams
I saw the girl with laughing eyes,
Whose skin shone silver like the moon,
Whose smile was like the rising sun,
And as she danced in honeysuckle haze
Beneath the diamond-spangled sky,
I lost my soul to pleasure-sigh.

LIKE WIND
Phil Billing.

Like wind-driven clouds we collide
And thunder our joy,
Flashing the iridescence of our souls
In sky-splitting flame-spitting arrows.

Like titans in leather and bronze,
Straddling the gentle mountains,
Roaring the lion of our hearts,
Shaking the foundations of the earth,
Waking the dragon.

Melt like the stars,
Chocolate over lips and dribble
Over brim and nibble
At the edge of cosmic pleasure.
Our voices, the deep shivering
Cello and the burning violin.

Leap of Love

Travis Blair.

Two yellow leaves
Let go and leap
In reckless abandon
From shaky branches.

One shows off
His floating somersaults,
Delights the other,
Who pirouettes
And claps her hands.

They swirl around,
Fandango dancing,
As Cupid's breeze
Directs their fall
Into a heap
On fallow ground.

She lands on top,
A gentle plop.
They roll and kiss,
Entwined and locked.

Intoxicated
In tumbling bliss,
They cling together
Until they stop.
She smiles and sighs,
And whispers softly:
"I knew it would
Feel like this."

A Fog Engulfed Kiss

Joshua Brownfield.

I slept with a new girl last night,
Met her in my dreams.
A dense white fog unveils for her presence,
A slight glow outlines her figure.
As I stand, leaning up against the cold
Limestone of a city landscape,
Smoking a menthol cigarette,
She passes me with a ghostly presence.
I turn my head to follow the sweet, cool air.
She marks molecules with a musical scent,
The inhalation makes my heart sing.
I drop my lit cigarette and follow.
The fog closes up around her,
holding her in its density,
Holding her tight, an impenetrable force.
I run after her, fighting through heavenly clouds.
She is lost, the fog has taken her from me.
Maybe she was escaping;
I just wanted to be her hero.
I turn around and take one step
In the opposite direction.
The tip of my Kenneth Cole shoe is trapped.

I look up and there she is,
Through the fog,
It's just her and me standing tip to tip,
Toe to toe.
Her hair is golden,
Streaming waves of light through
The dark empty holes in my eyes,
Enlightening,
Her eyes full of fawn awakening.
She is soft as a tender petal.
I swirl the tips of my fingers
Across her pale, silky back,
Up the valley of smooth flesh cradling her spine,
All the way up to her tender lips
Percolating with pleasure awaiting.
I kiss her once and lean back,
watching and waiting, her eyes closed,
Those long lashes stroked with mascara, elongating.
They open, I want then to.
I want them to see me coming close,
Coming close to a fog engulfed kiss.

THE ART OF
TURNING HEADS

Travis Blair.

Amy, over pasta pollo
And a vintage Chardonnay,
Smiles like a feral feline,
Purrs in my ear, "Maybe, Baby,
This will lift your spirits."
Rising from the table, practiced
At the art of turning heads,
She slow-walks across the room,
Sultry like a wet dream,
Glancing over shoulder to see
If I am watching her.
Every eye at Terilli's follows the
Rhythmic motion of her hips.
The aroma of desire rises like
Smoke rings in the air,
As conversation ceases
And wives become invisible.
Looks of envy dart my way

And I sit taller in my chair,
Facing a hundred looters ready
To kill or die for her beauty.
Ships set sail like pirates coming
to pillage my sylphlike treasure.
She returns to me navigating
Shark infested waters and
Plants a kiss on my lips.
Waves rise high in the storm sea,
Toppling over ships and crushing
Any man who's hopes are still live.
As we exit the café,
My arm around her waist,
She laughs and asks
If I feel better, and I smile
All the way to the harbor
Of our waiting bed.

LOVE SONG

Janice Windle.

I sat
sweating in my July hat
your leg warm on mine,
your smile glowing near my cheek,
your song, that I fancied only I could hear,
opening my heart like a flower
to the sun.
"Come, come,
No harm can be done
If I sculpt with my hands
Your curving hips;
With my tongue, part
Your waiting lips;
Reframe your sexuality
So that it's powered by
Our loving needs."
And all the heated day
I'm falling, falling, falling,
believing you will catch me
in your soft net....

THAT NIGHT
Janice Windle.

That night
without warning,
without suspicion,
without demands,
we folded together
like a book and its cover
and you were my lover.

FEASTING
Janice Windle.

To sip, to sip, never to drain the cup;
To stroke with gentle lip, to savour
Slowly, slowly, tasting every flavour
That flickering tongue and loving hand yields up.

THE STANDARD ISSUE UNIFORM
Morgan Nichols.

She met him at a grey interval
in her life: the blue skies
didn't tell her much.

In the corner where love and hate
mix, she chose both:
the standard issue didn't suit
that well, but it was an old favourite.

She met him over a sneaky beer,
not her usual civilised glass of wine.
The band oozed heat
into the crevices of her armpits:
she worried frantically about body odour

and their conversation splayed its arms into the future,
a future where he knew her well
enough to pee with the door open,
and she could bitch to her friends
without guilt.

But now, the choice was clearly
in front of her: and as he
leaned over to ask her name
she felt the familiar thud of excitement:

Like the echo of their future son's
basketball in an empty court.

Flower In The Rain

Kurt Rees.

We met for lunch,
and after some short conversation
I looked outside.
It began to rain.
I smiled with relief and told her,
"It's a good thing I got
the flowers planted earlier."
She smiled and told me,
"Flowers shine much brighter
in the rain. The rain washes away
the dirt and brings the color out."

After lunch and some conversation,
I walked her to the front
of the restaurant.
She covered her head
and walked out the door.
I saw her through the glass
of the door as she
turned to me.
She smiled
and blew me a kiss.

I smiled back
as she ran through the rain
to her car.
She was right.
Flowers do shine brighter
in the rain.

MATCH THE PACE

Kurt Rees.

We lie in bed.
Her deep green eyes
like emerald pools
glaring at me.
The full moon
beams through the window,
dancing across her long blonde hair.
She tells me she loves me.
My body weak,
I can only believe.
My hand slowly moves
along her silky skin,
gliding across curves,
curves that would bring
any man to his knees.
My heart beats faster
as she smiles at my touch.
How could God make
such a beautiful woman?
Her hand touches my face
and she slowly moves closer.
Our lips touch,
bodies tangled in moonlight.
A kiss,
a kiss of passion,
love,
lust.

It is then
I feel her heartbeat
match the pace of mine.

SCRUFFY

Simon Philbrook.

I went down to Covent Garden
To listen to the cappuccino machines.
I watched the scruffy lovers
playing beatnik tricks.
They wore tackety kick-about boots
Tied up with string.

She sang,
as he tapped out a tune
on his tatty old acoustic.
It rained,
It rained on their peaked black caps
and their odd socks.
They stole kisses from the rain.

I watched,
I watched as
the touch-torn lovers,
the lip-bitten lovers,
the scruffy lovers,
kissed,
touched,
loved.

Tumble down days
Made tatty with love.
What we are
is love.

IS IT A LOVE POEM?

Puma Perl.

Is it a love poem because instead of my usual garden
salad I steamed some snow peas, added mango slices,
slivered almonds, sun dried tomatoes, and two kinds of greens?
Is it a love poem because I always sleep with four fluffy
pillows and soft sheets and I fell out pretty quick in a tent
with two blankets on the ground and a rolled up sweatshirt
under my head and then I peed behind a tree?
Is it a love poem because I said love poem when I usually write
blood heroin cracked pavement garbage street words and
I'm writing stuff like slivered almonds and love poem?
Is it a love poem because I didn't want gifts wrapped in Hallmark
for my birthday and I got everything I wanted, naked and
unwrapped?

Is it a love poem because instead of typing it on a cold computer
I have a craving for the smell of ink, a desire to write in ornate
script on lined paper, elegantly embossed, sealed in gold?
Is it a love poem because random guys smile at me and pass
me their numbers because guys always know when someone
else is getting something good and they want some too?
Is it a love poem because despite the fact that this may be a
love poem I think about love mostly when I'm making it
and have a lot of other stuff to think about the rest of the time?
Is it a love poem because I've finally learned only to
ask questions when I'm ready to handle answers?
Is it a love poem because when someone shows me exactly who
they are I believe them? Is it a love poem because I'm pretty
sure where I end and everyone else begins, except in moments
that I don't write about because they are already love poems?

Is it a love poem?

I think maybe it is but I don't write love poems so perhaps it is
not....
but there is a softness in my eyes and desire in the words I choose.

I have written a poem.....
Is it a love poem?

NOURISH ME

Art Noble.

Nourish my body with cookin'
As your love nourishes my soul.
Fix me Southern Fried Chicken,
Mashed potatoes with lumps,
So I know they're real.
You can even leave skins on.
Sawmill gravy to cover them,
And well cooked string beans
With fat back, or country fried.
And sweet, soft corn bread
With butter meltin' on the top.
Maybe one of those fine apple pies
With little fork holes that say,
"I love you" in the crust.

TINY QUAKE

Susan Morgan Bosler.

It was just a tiny quake
that quickly grew,
the ground under my feet
undulating like a snake,
a boat on the ocean
cresting on the tip of a wave,
a generous serving of "suddenly,"
the rapid beating of a heart,
the breaths that turned to panting,
the sound that broke the silence,
the freight train moving
through the world taking
down everything in its path.

Then it stopped,
all stopped,
the silence broken by the crashing
of glass upon concrete,
the alarms of cars,
the cries of babies,
the shouting of men,
arrant sirens,
helicopters overhead.

Fawning, laughing,
I realized I was alive
and that was only
our first kiss.

LIKE THAT

Cyndi Dawson.

It wasn't like that. He wasn't.
So much of it didn't.
She really couldn't.
Yet it came together.

Spaces filled in. Words took their seats.
The New York skyline nestled
Into the background of Jersey City.
It all... quite suddenly.

Jack Daniels-smooth, steady...
She started to. He was.
Then they decided...
Everything. Right now.

The air on the pier, cool,
As the East River rippled against
Wood planks. He held her tight;
This was. They were.

THE EIGHTH WONDER
OF THE WORLD
Misha.

Sitting in such awe,
awareness through osmosis,
it is not your words, nor your deeds,
it is the openness of your heart
that has given me these wings.
Outstretched palm, home,
I am given freedom beyond what
weak poetic ramblings
could ever tell.
I simply sit
speechlessly alive within
your love.

AN ECSTATIC GIFT
OF A LUNATIC
Misha.

I travelled to the moon
and brought you this rock.
It may not seem like much
more than a symbol
hard to decipher, a foreign concept
to wrap your mind around,
this one of a kind gift, this treasure,
in your hand the heft of weightlessness,
curl sensitive tips round lunar ground,
imagine the bounce contained within
a journey amongst the stars,
an adventure into a familiar face,
land your mind within mine and feel
the spacelessness of space,
distances spanned here, ecstatic wonder
beyond symbolism of any kind.

Descriptions miss the mark
so I brought you back a rock.

Come on,
let's skip it.
We'll count rings of the ripple.

A Word With You

Misha.

If I had a word
with you
it would

be.

If I had two words
with you
they would

be
one.

If I had three words
with you
they would

be
one
love.

If I had four words
with you
they would

be
one
love
still.

If I had five words
with you
they would

be
two more
than necessary.

Your Hands

Robin Miller.

I watch you wave your hands
through the air as you speak
and become jealous of the air they caress.
I bet the space they move through
yields at your command.
Your palms are large but it seems
your fingers would be longer to match.
I wonder if this is because
you are better at holding things
than greedily grasping for them.
How do you keep them so soft?
I really don't understand.
I know you are mostly at a computer
all week in the office,
but as a weekend warrior
with wheelbarrows and lawn mowers,
I would have guessed you had
at least a callous or two.
Then I remember your heart,
and I know your hands are the same.
My own heart rests in them,
even and perhaps especially
when they are tangled up in my hair.

WIND LOVED FIRE

Robin Miller.

Your wind touches my flame
and I swell into an ardent blaze
brilliant with fortitude
in the face of my final consternation.
It could not be confronted until
I was cloaked with the armor of your
gracious and unremitting devotion.
There is nothing more priceless
in this expensive world than the
license your confidence in me affords.
You give me the gift of I Can.
You will be blessed, my king, with I Am...
I Am your queen who draws her sword
at the spectre who lurks and tries to
steal the kismet of the kiss
courage leaves on my brow.
I Am forever at your service,
not in debt, but in gratitude
for how you expand my latitude of light
and coil me into the might of my own heat.

WHEN WINTER COMES

Robin Miller.

When winter comes
I will look back on these fiery days
and remember the turning
of the summer skies
into the fall leaves
scratching on the asphalt
and I will hear the roar of
the ocean in them.
I will wish for snow,
wrap myself in a throw
and love the cold,
slumbering world bigger than ever.

When winter comes
I will be glad
that I embraced this summer
in the best way possible –
by embracing you.
I have dug my heels
into the sand of my
best loved love
and learned to laugh
in the face of the rising mercury.

When winter comes
I will warm you
with my constant love
and unyielding passion
for this sweet, sweet life,
as you have warmed me,
even on my cold, cold
summer days.

A TRADE OF HEARTS
Davis Luther.

How softly she comes,
unnoticed
like a breeze into my life.

If not for the soft brush against my cheek
I would have never turned to look.

But with that gaze
a frozen moment,
a lifetime of loneliness…

vanished…

in a trade
of
hearts.

HAPPINESS

Liselotte Holm.

I'm holding my breath
So close to your breath
You can carry it in our kiss.

Holding your breath inside me
Is like holding you
In me.

Buckle the little space-bubble in me
Where you live
In a tummy-sparkle.

And just to tease you
I will squeeze you
Happy too.

I'm flying in your delight,
I'm trying to enter the night,
I'm spying on it,
I'm relying on it,
I'm trying to make it right,
I'm trying to cater the light,
To make you glow tonight.

The night is coming to invade us,
To sweep us off our feet,
And by intensifying our inverted gloom,
Transmute us.

How nice is the night,
Dazzling images of unlit dreams.
So, touch the darkest matter in the darkest room
With the tip of your tongue.

Explore The Darkness,
Venture further than the end

Of the black matter,
Stumble on space.

Sing out the Song of all songs,
My Dawn.

SOUL MATES?

Fran Hoffpauir.

Soul mates. Define that, if you please.
Sensing each other in a far-off breeze?
Finishing one another's every thought?
A telepathy the universe has wrought?
A touch that conducts an electric spark?
A joy in sight that glows in the dark?
A pain so intense it's near sublime?
A love so deep it surpasses all time?
From all I can fathom, it's all the above.
It's touch, smell, sound, lust and love.

LOVE ALONG THE WAY

Shelley Haggard.

As strong as our grip, as delicate as our love,
is the lacy ice that mates the edge of water to the sand.
We walk beside the Fraser River, fingers twined,
my smaller bones sheltered in your strong hand.

Crow calls lead our ears to an arriving flock of geese,
mate alongside mate flying in a V for Valentine form.
The geese come through the mountains down into the
valley, to land with their love and feed in a farmer's field.

Their trumpeted love song gives way to an eagle's call,
and the answering call from its mate in a tree;
powerful wings fold so that he might join her
to watch us as we pass by underneath.

All is well when I can smell your skin touched by wind,
and I can see the promise of spring in your eyes of green.
I feel my heartstrings pulled until my love overflows.
Walking in this world beside you, I feel reawakened:
dreamed.

All I ask is that you hold on to me tightly!
Hold me so I don't grow old and distant like the
mountains!

Touch your lips to mine and prove once more
that your heart and soul, like mine, are open.

FROM CROWN TO BASE

Shelley Haggard.

(Composed from the words and phrases from the poem:
"The Ballad of the Northern Lights" by Robert Service.)

I bore the famine of love handily;
but when I met her, I lost my head at the feast.
My heart beat a cotillion so intricate
I thought surely it would burst.

I spied around her a corona of flame,
bright enough to melt the haggard Arctic heights.
Alabaster skin that begged my touch; a beauty
like needles of stars that stabbed my eyes.

Slowly, in a silent, silvered solitude,
we danced a devil-dance across bruised-silk snow.
Reckless spirits of fierce revolt
we lay down upon her cloak.

The mighty river, Passion, snatched us up
and bore us swift along. In perfect chorus
we claimed the air and ground
with our sweet and keening song.

The sky; a giant scythe, scooped up our love
into pennants of silver to wave:
to be counted among the souls before us
who were once so brave and so naïve.

And later, in the tallow's gleam, we played on the game.
I was her Knight of the Hollow Needle, and she,
The Northern Queen.

If the entire world should darken – should retire the hosts of fire:
we could light the night and light the day, so strong is our desire.

I Will Always Love
You Like This

Geraldine Green.

I will always love you like this,
the way a tree loves the sky,
the way a man loves his fishing line,
the way a tractor dwells on the land,
sighing and ploughing each deep furrow,
veining the earth, turning over coins,
angels dreams and kombolois.

I will always love you like this,
the way a horse slowly chews its oats,
the way a river tumbles over grand canyons,
the way a sky bleeds itself
into the ocean at sunrise.

I will always love you like this,
in the slow dance of mayflies over a river,
in the way a salmon leaps
upstream to spawn each spring,
the way geese return to the tundra.

I can hear their wings beating the air,
I can hear your heart beating against me
as I lie on your chest in the winter in our home,
in the summer in the bivvy,
on the fells under bracken, inside mansions,
by the ocean, in the clouds sometimes,
like gods squabbling.
Then kiss!
A quick smile, a hug, a make up, an ok!
So I apologise.
I love you and will always love you.
Right now. Just like this.

DARK EYES

Patricia Carragon.

I dived into your storm,
Swam along currents
Of dark brown.
We wrote our history
Under a blanket,
And in a flash
Love needed no explanation.

THE CORNEAL GATES

Patricia Carragon.

You keep my image
Behind corneal gates.
I look closer,
See an hourglass
Where sand becomes
An endless beach –
Where a shell lies
Like a castaway.

I pick it up,
Hear thoughts sing,
Watch notes rise
Like fire's breath.
I ask the wind
To send this song
To where dreams live,
Wait for his eyes
To open the gates.

FEELING AURORAS

Heather Moon Sofran.

We feel auroras.
We sit out on the deck in the dark,
You and I.
We bathe in summer's humid breath,
In reclining blue beach chairs,
And listen to the night bugs whirring
Their last-ditch love songs,
Slowly sipping drinks trickling cold
Drops of condensation on our chests.
We gaze up and out
Beyond the blanket of atmosphere
And wait.
Every night we do this
No matter what the season,
Ever since that one freezing night
When we saw them overhead,
Drifting by in liquid gauze ribbons
And pulsing, nebulous starbursts
Of ethereal aqua light.
We stayed until we were numb,
Our minds forever touched
By magnetism glowing.
Though the sky doesn't lift
Her veils and dance tonight,
You tilt your head toward mine and ask,
"Do you feel them?"
I smile and nod because I do.
We feel auroras.

LOVE IS NOT A CHOICE

Heather Moon Sofran.

We stop by the symphony house
Tonight, where rain and doves sing
Clear and sweet and concrete free.

In the garden fairy's
Dewy little theatre
I ask you to please stay with me
Just a moment longer,
To glide easily together
Among ancient, rusty coffee cans,
Water-logged bowling balls
And homemade wind chimes
Of yarn and hollow reeds.

You nod your assent
With gentleness in your eyes.

I rest my hand on your thigh,
Warming your leg and my hand
As we watch birds flitting
And sipping water from dripping leaves
With delicate, lily-petal tongues.

This is the enchanted moment I need,
An instant of synchronized serenity
To tell you I love you,
But the words crumble in my throat
And come out as great puffs of vapour,
Like the cows' bellows breath
In the wet field beside us.

I am aware that one day
I'll run out of chances,
But, as we listen to the rain
I am drowning on I love you,
And despite my gagged silence,
We are both immersed
In what it is I can't say.

FALLING THROUGH
THE CRACKS
Jillian Parker.

I saved up all of my love poems for so long
they wore holes in my pockets
and then words began to trip me up
on the way out the door.

Couplets fell into my coffee
and when I showered
cascades of alliteration
slurped down the drain.

So they might be a bit lumpy,
over-ripe or fermented,
but if you ever have need of them
I'll send them all to you –

A DREAM
Jillian Parker.

A lemon-scented lampada, throwing
rouge shadows onto a holy image:

I am the whiff of feather-touch,
I am the silence of sighs,
I am the hovering mist,
I am the ribbon trembling.

You are the words in the wind,
You are a fortress of tact,
You are the wisdom of amber,
You are washed by a salt sea

into an azure trance ...

REFLECTION

Carol Voccia.

Speak to me in deepest true,
Gather me up like a silk napkin and blot me across
Tendered words dripped from lips purging.
Let me absorb all you wish to say,
Wrapped attention to your meaning
Of worried doubts; jagged edged world dividing,
Soaking you of strength and reasoned mind.
Still the music you feign to sing
Strums beneath the soul,
The harp plucking to be heard.
I'll hear you
And wrap winged thoughts as gauzed bandage,
Rock you in all the pleasures your depth can hold,
Care not your wilted garden,
Thorned bush or jilted path,
Let me take up your brightness in a porcelain cup
And sip from it until you're mirrored in my eyes.

SINGING FALSETTO

Michéle Vassal-Ring.

today I will wear my canary yellow bra the one that sings
falsetto on my skin
today I will spice my thighs with patchouli and rose
today I will musk the hollows of my clavicles
today I will kohl my eyes Egyptian
today I will paint my lips coral buds
today I will scent my breath with cardamom
today I will reap armfuls of irises and elder flowers for the
green glass vase
today I will make a daub marinated in Cahors, smoothed
with tapenade
today I will roast peppers with anchovies and open a
bottle of that violet wine
today I will brush the cat and wash the dog and dance
away dust and cobwebs
today I will cleave time into instants rounded and
gleaming like spheres of mercury
today I will not be sad
today I will not be mad
today I will not frown
today I will not think of "her"
today I will not talk about "then"
today I will not go to black or even grey
today I will pyrotechnic you
today I will Versailles you
today I will necromance you
today I will wait for you.

PASSIONS IGNITE
Patricia Allen.

The candle sparks wildly,
your skin glows with musk,
I tenderly touch you,
we mutually trust.

Your lips burn with passion,
my tongue cools the flame,
our hearts feed the embers,
that no rule can tame.

Inhibitions run rampant,
we dare to display,
our nakedness plainly,
in pure light of day.

Passions ignited,
true love takes her stand,
two lovers united,
one woman, one man.

LOVERS

Sam Brannon.

Lovers...
With only good intentions for the other,
Nothing about their time together is cheap or fake.
They Love because it is the greatest thing they know to make.
Brought together by the Universe' great hand,
This woman... this man.

Together...
For now, but not forever,
By grand design they each have things to do and see.
By staying true to perfect Love they remain free.
They've both kept their sacred Universal vow,
To be here... together... now.

They part...
Both richer of the heart,
Though far removed by physics' space and time,
Their bond is of the class known as sublime.
When two people come together in perfect Love
That is enough.

LAST NIGHT

Tere-Jo Buckingham.

Laughter,
Smiles,
Joy,
Filled the room.
Conversation,
Light hearts,
Expression,
A fun time embraced the room.
Friends,
Strangers,
All of us one,
A great time in one room.
Simple,
Eloquent,
Beautiful,
People in one room.
Giggles,
Happiness,
Love.
Filled the room.

LOVE

Lauren Eulalie Parker.

your acid secret
you are the connection
with bribes so pleasant

as you assault the dreaming
brew a mad love potion
the grandeur of singing
an opal
you are awakened by an ice-water bath

the sepia photographs thoughtfully hang on the wall
dreamy you spin like a pinwheel
your self-indulgence unfolds

lust gives away to white ideas
curly-haired girls and their polished surface

she drinks like a fish
I am a silver-bullet child
talking in blotches of bright colour

drown in wet glitter
your withered terror
of a blissful life
is more than you can bare

the knife found in the woodshed
glittery knife

you were dizzying
as I read my contemplative fairytales
the telephone on the wall
silence had cracked
your grin is all I see through the smoke
calm tempo
for the crashing oblivion

A MOMENT STILLED?
Matthew Griffiths.

Every moment seems so precious,
Every second spent with thee,
Oh to stop the ticking clock now,
And together simply be.

With thy cheek against my fingers,
Softest skin in warm caress,
Like our hearts at once united,
Bound in ways that none could guess.

And thy gentle rhythmic breathing,
Brings a calmness to my soul,
For 'tis only when I'm with thee,
That I feel completely whole.

Not a word need be spoken,
For our spirits soar in song,
As immersed within each other,
We both know we belong.

Let me drink in every facet,
Of thy beauty and thy grace,
As I revel in the moment
That we share true love's embrace

SENSUAL RHAPSODY

Naome James.

His finger tenderly crosses
the bridge of her nose,
thumb slightly brushing her lips,
his lips gently kissing her closed,
coherent eyes,
as the warmth of his breath
wafts their sighs,
caressing the crescents of her waves,
revealing the midriff
and the rising passion,
anticipation, craving,
diving deep into her ocean,
carried by desire's crest
to drift among the ripples
and descend to the wade-pools
of nostalgia.

THE ROSE

Catherine Rose.

I overlooked the blushing daisy,
instead, deconstructed the rose,
counting each dusk-kissed pearly petal
as it drifted down to stroke the floor:

he loves me,
he loves me not,
he loves me,
he loves me not,
he loves me.

I forgot the blues of the forget-me-not,
instead, gently wrote a syncopated love note
on every soft-lipped satin heart,
to launch skywards and shower him
in some invisible future,
like a dream of confetti.

I, THE PAINTER

Anna Savage.

I painted you with my own inner brush,
My sable haired seduction rush,
I dabbed at your edges with a soft oiled cloth,
and lovingly added Titanium White
To sparkle your sad, young, yearning eyes,
and highlight your peachy, dusky skin.
Sure, I'm being polite,
But then, I was so proud,
And isn't that what love is all about?

I, the painter:
I painted you into my inner sketch book
In glowing ochre colours
that would make other girls sigh, scowl,
and even die with envy.
I store you here,
like a water-colour-tipped bowl of fruit
that posed especially for the occasion
the afternoon.

And you?
I saved you on my much loved natural canvas
in the personal studio of my future dreams,
and wrapped it in the well worn
expensive leather-smelling portfolio
of my heart.

Then I, the painter,
was offered a good price for you.
But this ruthlessly schooled
sentimental young fool,
Never really equipped
to make a proper living,
could not bring herself
to sell you on,
could not bear to accept payment
for this priceless thing so fine,
that in the end
did not seem like mine.

Post Modern Romance

Chuck Steffan.

I stand
Before you
Stark naked,
Completely exposed,
My heart wide open,
Pleading its case.

Give me something
To hold onto
When I grow old.
Tell me you'll
Love me until
The end of time.

Give me a tenderness
I hardly know
Anymore,
Make love to me
Like it's
The end of the world.

My Heart Has Room For No One Else

Irene Jardalla.

Did you think I would forget you,

Your memory wouldn't stay?

Did you think I would stop caring

The second you went away?

That would never happen, sweetest,

That I would never do -

My heart has room for no one else,

For it's full of love for you.

BESIDE ME

Michele A. Spano Krenza.

In the harsh steel light of daybreak
skyscrapers stand tall
when words are cold and people few...
life's cruel burdens crashing down...

Come lay beside me,
grasp a twinkling of the day,
serenity we'll hold ,
eyes gazing, lending hope,
caressing warm
this heart with broken wings.

When stars cast tiny shimmers
in the cold, cold dead of night,
and demons cloak ghostly
memories beneath our fears,
and all that's left is loneliness...

Come lay beside me,
grasp a twinkling of the day,
serenity we'll hold.
Gentle hands reach out
embracing warmly
this heart with broken wings.

When storms are fast and manifold,
and skies bleed ominous wounds,
compose the seas, ebb the tides,
lay beside me for a twinkling of a day.

Serenity we'll own,
settle troubles,
cause to ease,
to hush...
to still this heart
with broken wings.

July Rain
Rudy Thomas.

The rain falling in the early
morning lures me
out of the A-frame.

The drizzle hits me
warm and wet. Silently,
I whisper your name.

Your memory becomes as rain.
I want to be naked
inside you.

Poem in the Afternoon
Rudy Thomas.

I think about you when rain begins.
I don't carry an umbrella.
Drops fall, sprinkles and little more.
I get damp as I walk.

I want you.
I want to write words across a page.
I want the words to be you.
It is possible.

I imagine rain falling
where you are. In my mind
you are a page
and I am crafting internal rhymes...

all afternoon.

The Beginning

Ellen Zaks.

Starry night of a thousand falls of light
reflecting and reflected in my pupils,
sky-black and huge,

you have executed
your soft spirals of chance
across the Milky Way.

Now dragged into the arms of the fir-trees,
the vanishing points are sustained
when I hold my breath.

In stillness
they grow large and unblinking.
The silence has terrifying immensity.

This ice-crackling grass,
this cold, this night,
begin their containment in memory.

Absolute reality
threatens to roll in
and unravel my beginning.

Boy

Dianne Arthur.

Remember when you asked me
about God, late at night
after the magnolia
waxed its pink
turned brown?

Your young blood,
your beauty;
we talked about cheese
and the moon.

On Sunday morning
you sent me a song,
Vermillion,
and I sent you
Rufus Wainwright back.

We spent all that day
together, last autumn,
me in Cornwall,
you in Hull,

but woke up alone
on Monday,
after the dreaming,
me barefoot in the garden
deadheading roses,

your long strides
down the orchard
past the apple trees
swept up in an embrace.

We had nothing to say
then,
just holding
and holding.

You

Ivan Woodberry.

You came to me unexpectedly,
Turning my life upside down.
You put the beat back into a dead heart
Right from the very start.
You turned my eyes from the darkness
Full of shadows and shades of grey.
While looking deep into your eyes
I saw the beauty that resides within.
Your soul shines like a bright star,
Showing just what and who you are.
You ripped away the darkness that lies
Deep within me, and
The tenderness you show
Fills my heart with love and joy.
Tears are in my eyes...
Eyes that were once unable to cry.
Now I can see the beauty in front of me.
It will always remain a part of me.
You are so near and yet so far away
I cannot touch you,
Wrap my arms around you,
Or hold your soft hands in mine,
While I tenderly kiss your lips
And run my fingers through your red hair.
Although our worlds are so far apart
You will always be at
The centre of my heart.

ANTICIPATION

Joyce Åkesson.

The universe has no centre,
The sky has no roots,
The space has a key,
The sun opens its arms,
The earth breathes,
A flower shakes its head,
Life has a perfume,
The walls shiver,
The roads dance,
The laughter has a special color,
The silence is moved,
The words flow,
An illusion makes us forget,
We dream of the truth,
Love keeps us awake.

Trap Door

John Hirst.

Life continues below, whilst
memories stagnate above.
Trap-door, a loft-lid to the attic.

Musty, stale, dank air escapes
as we rescue our Yuletide
decorations for seasonal parole.

Torch beams search out shapes,
sad silhouettes of a generation lost,
promises broken, keepsakes discarded.

Relics of a now so very distant past,
dusty, rusty baby paraphernalia,
mouldy, discarded failed-career memorabilia.

Soft cuddly toys with long forgotten names,
wife's wedding dress, an incubated archive.
Blissful Start - Blood Ties - Happy Ending.

Faded pink, faint-perfumed envelopes,
SWALK-marked, forever and ever yours.
Ageing Rhetoric - Perfect Parchment -Lights On.

My Love

Connie Anderson.

You nodding by the fire,
I take down a special
book and slowly read,
and dream of the soft look
your eyes had once,
and of their shadows deep.

So many loved your presence
of strength, full of grace;
they loved your passion for life and faith,
and I, I loved the very soul in you,
and loved the sorrows
of your changing face.

And bending down beside the glowing embers,
I quietly and sadly say, how love fled each year,
fading ever so slowly. You let go....
Yet, I would know your face amid a crowd of stars.

FIFTY YEARS OF LOVE
NEVER ENDING

Angelyn C Haynes.

(Dedicated to Angelyn's grandparents:
Della Ann Cairnes Maurer & John Anton Maurer).

They spent over fifty years just loving,
sharing and caring for one another.
They spent every minute of every day together,
showing their love for each other.
They were devoted to and saw only each other.
Theirs was a loving friendship,
and they were lovers in dark of night.
The simple things kept their love alive,
their romance coming from heart, body, soul and mind.
A simple flower brought by him from her flower bed,
a special dinner she worked on all day,
prepared for him to enjoy by candle light.
There were walks in the moonlight, holding hands,
and, as the years went by their love never wavered,
it just grew stronger and greater.
They lived like there was no tomorrow,
loved each other with heart and soul,
made love by the light of the moon,
cared for each other when sick,
and shared all their thoughts and desires,
desires of passion, flames of wanting.
To them, loving someone meant forever.
Their vow: To have and to hold from this day forward
was sacred; they honoured that vow with a kiss,
and fifty years of wedded bliss.

I HAVE NOT FORGOTTEN
HOW LOVELY YOU ARE
Phil Billing.

I have not forgotten how lovely you are.
I have not taken memories,
Folded them neatly
And stored them safely away
In the cupboard that I never open.
I have not turned,
And in reverse
Sped out along the road of regret.
I have not unwanted what I have had,
And I cannot untaste what I have tasted,
Nor unlove what I have loved.
I have not forgotten.
I will not forget,
No,
I will remember
And savour the memory,
And I will smile at your rainbow love
Stretched across the sky.

ALONG THE COASTAL TRAIL

Phil Billing.

Along the coastal trail,
Between the wide beach
Or the stony bluffs
Rising ruggedly,
Defiant against wind and wave,
And the tidy lines of date palms
Still as porcelain,
Straight as soldiers,
Unbroken slabs of rock
Lie flat and dark, one upon another,
Like gargantuan blocks of bitter chocolate
Carpeted with luminous kelp
That glows and fades
With the swell and fall of tide.

I cannot help but feel your presence here,
Where sunken sky meets silver sea
In a fever mist.

I cannot help but run with joy
Beside your ocean smile,
Skipping light in the wake of your voice.

RAIN

Phil Billing.

I didn't think for a moment
That you would come.

Too often I have stood alone,
Wavering,
Revolving in subdued anticipation,
Waiting in vain,
Flicking my wrist
To check again the slow-ticking time,
Watching the feet of passers-by.

But you are here now, with me,
In this happy thunder moment,
When the bloated clouds break
And the rain falls like laughter
And we are drenched
And dizzy.

And I smile…
Because we have no umbrella.

DEATH BY SEDUCTION

Travis Blair.

She sat
languid as sin
at an outdoor table,
one leg stretched straight,
and on it
a razor-toed boot
made of striped
python skin,

some once-powerful
Amazon serpent
who'd spent his life
seducing prey,
crushing the life out
of them, but now
content as ornament
for her long shapely leg.

And it was then
that I realized the power
this woman wielded,
sizing me up for her game,
and I felt my breath
squeezed out of me
and knew the thrill
of death by seduction.

TWELVE DEGREES
FROM FREEZING
Travis Blair.

Somewhere south of faith, I stood
twelve degrees from freezing,
cloaked in my self-pity robe,
my broken spirit bleeding.
Out of nowhere came a hand,
that pulled me from the dark,
led me gently from my pain,
and pressed me to its heart.

A heart that wrapped me in its love,
and warmed my frozen soul,
kissed away my darkest fears,
healed and made me whole.

I don't know what you saw in me
that made me seem worth saving,
nor why you gave me all your love,
I find it so amazing.

But I believe in me again,
and this I know is true,
as long as life exists in me,
I owe it all to you.

IF NOT FOR LOVE

Janice Windle.

If you and I had never met and loved,
My heart would be a tight black bud,
Forever furled, seeming to be promising
A fragrant opening, a spreading bed of roses,
But closed, bitten early by the frost,
Closed forever, sterile, without love.

If my eyes had never opened on your clear gaze,
My blindness, my oblivion, would be complete.
Wrapped in night I'd not have seen my future,
My past and every moment of my present,
Bathed in rose light, glowing,
Softly coloured by the lens of love.

If I had not heard your voice
Murmuring close, crying out in passion,
Making of my name a holy mantra,
I'd not have known what music is,
Nor listened to my inner voice
That prompts my songs of everlasting love.

If I had not smelled your skin's perfume,
Nor tasted sweetness on your morning breath,
Nor pressed my head to your broad chest
And breathed musk through the warm damp wool,
I'd still live in a desert place, without
The sweet-sour scents that we create through love.

If with loving hands I had not touched
Your hands that bring such ecstasy to me,
Not stroked the velvet secrets that you hide,
Nor felt your gentle mouth upon my breast,
My body'd be a prison and a shell,

If you and I had never lain in love.

VISION

Janice Windle.

Back from the edge of the world,
where we in each other's arms have travelled,
I wake and see your face
outlined beside me on the pillow.

Your pale hair, back-flowing, flame-formed,
is the hair of Gabriel
in a painting of Apocalyptic heaven,
streaming from your oblique forehead, your profile aligned
and focused forward,
nose strangely delicate in this soft light,
mouth a fine line
compressed by flight through the black starry void,
chin drawn back by pressure of your impetus to Earth.

Or is this the face of a mediaeval knight,
carved in cold stone,
laid in a cool crypt far underground?
But as I look, you waken and are back with me:
my soldier-lover, beloved, but certainly no angel.

THE FRAME

Kurt Rees.

She came over again
and looked at the photo
in the old pewter frame.
A family member
near and dear
is what she sees.
I'm glad she doesn't know
the history of the frame:
all the old girlfriends
that showed smiles
through the glass,
now buried memories
in a drawer.
My favorite frame,
always in view of everyone
that walks in.
Hopefully, one day
her smile will grace the frame,
and I trust she understands
how big of a deal it is to me.

SONG OF THE LAST GIANT

Simon Philbrook.

Now is not the time to mourn,
for the oceans are not deep enough to hold our tears.

I heard a song.
It was the song of the last giant,
wailing and echoing through the depths of the Atlantic.
He sang of loneliness.
We who do not know love
have not touched such cold depths.
Our love is desire, and lust, and having,
getting and having.
Our love is red with pain.

The song of the last giant echoes the sounds of the sky,
water and fire, elemental beauty,
no stumbling words.
We, the tongue tripped have no song.
We are mute.

He sang of the first dawns,
when time was young and the music of the giants
filled the oceans,
when there was air to breath
and the rivers did not run with the blood of our wars
and the sting of our chemicals.
He sang of pain, wounds cut deep by our greed,
we who do not know love.
He sang of despair, that gifts are lost,
and love is dead, and we who do not know love
cannot grieve its death.

He sang of love,
in colours we have no eyes to see,
with music we cannot hear.
He sang of love and my heart burst
with the beauty of his song.

CONCERTO AMORE'
Art Noble.

I tune her fine orchestra,
crafted by dance, toned with labor.
Cleaning it first, oiling her every instrument,
her lines glisten in softened light.
Like the maestro tucking Strad. under chin,
she is delicately bed positioned,
while feathered bow is slowly drawn
across her muted strings.
For in this concerto, the first movement
is always largo.

Her body's tense vibrato augments
clean tones of the Concerto Amore'.
Her hungry instruments writhe in adagio and the
theme changes from piccolo to clarinet.
The maestro's smooth fingers prance and stroke
valves and keys and holes,
while his lips at her reed provide the power
to generate this vivace song.

Accelerando, maestro and orchestra become
as one he conducts the woodwinds,
fondling the snares, clutching the tympani,
kissing the lobes of her lute.
His presto oboe gracefully brings
a symphonic climax to her glowing orchestra.

Ritardando, the maestro gently holds her
in his arms for the tender coda.

She whispers,
"Encore! Encore!"

BEAUTIFUL MIRACLE

Cyndi Dawson.
(For Chelsea.)

The roots of her limbs;
The landscape of her
ever-changing form...
The light of darkness
lifted
as she
recreates me in her
ethereal innocence...

From a child rises
another
who grows the mother
and not vice-versa.
Life begins.
My beautiful miracle.

WATER WAYS
Misha.

Beauty sings!

As love birthed
by love mating
with love for life
undulates and arches
in the giving and receiving
waves of wonder.

Wild wisdom
spreads itself thickly
not to be missed.

Smiles split inside out
and into everything.

Unity is known because it is so
and nothing else is.

The ultimate eternal 'Oh'
silently awaits all those willing
to surrender into its watery ways,
leaving outdated identities behind
before stepping upon the shoreline
to swim in synchronicity's own swell.

Joy is buoyant
faith the sun
that lights the way a'sparkle and aha!

Gratitude grants grace,
lifting the limits of time and space,
a never ending free swim.

Laughter rolls with relish,
a healing hold on hearts held high,
wholly in service to the love birthed by love
mating with love
for life.

THIS IS A POEM
Misha.

This is a poem without limits.
This is a free flowing living moment to be within the Ah.
This poem has wings to fly into now and wrap us into
our most savored self, the holy one, the pure one, the
divine one.

This poem will not tell you anything you don't already know.
You know everything.
I have nothing new to say,
I have only this drive within to spill,
to spew, to water, to paint, to sculpt, to unpen,
to fly, to sing, to birth, to be
in that moment we love so well.

Now,
heaven is not a place,
heaven is a shared state of mind,
it is a knowing that is a given,
it is an otherworldly light with good reason,
it is beyond reason;
heaven asks for nothing in return
because we are there already,

we never left,
we are just master pretenders.

So let's pretend the key is in your pocket.
Look for the one marked willingness,
it fits the locks in the doors blocking
awareness of love.
Use it to unlock and open.

You know this love already,
it is not only your birthright, it is your true identity.
Like a superhero in a handmade costume you forgot,
but then you remembered and reminded me.
It is with gratitude I will sing into infinity
for as long as endless beginnings endure in timelessness.

Now,
join with me, we are not two as one,
we are one as one has always been,
the original lover, the original friend.
Glory be to our creator, perfection
has God's own name and it is Love.

EAGER HUNGRY KISS

Robin Miller.

If ever I was not amazed by you
I am sorely sorry.
Lusty magic is back in the air
and I'm sucking it in
as fast as I can.
Always below the surface of things
there are giant waves of luscious life
waiting to be slowly licked off the spoon
sitting on my plate of pearls.
I am teased by your big astound.
I am caressed by the stillness
of your God peering into my eyes
through the gaze of a tall touchy tree.
I roll the air I breathe over my tongue
and find my breath
an insufficient substitute
for your mouth.
I don't know where my bashful went.
It ran away when you came.
Whatever this is, my old lover,
let's welcome it to our hearth
and embrace it with an
eager hungry kiss.

The Deep End

Robin Miller.

Small flock of two
splashing in the pool,
laughing and chatting
in the day before summer sun.
You light the sky with your smile
while I go under
holding my breath.
We float quietly on our backs.
The water serenades.
Our heartbeats accompany
this enclave moment of attention
and awe that collects us back from
the frenetic flow of things.
The brief space between us carries
meaning only you and I understand.
Silence and pauses are like that.
They bring us to the million voices
Siddhartha heard in the river
that hummed, like us, the holy Om.

Transformative

Robin Miller.

One morning you will wake up.
You will wonder how you ever lived
without such fullness of joy,
and in the same moment
be glad you have known such sorrow.
It is true that grief carves out a canyon within
that bliss does eventually come to fill.
You will stand at the kitchen window
gazing at the indigo blue of six a.m.
and marvel at how far you have come;
at how deep your river has begun to run.
You will listen to something simple,
like the sound of a percolating coffee pot,
or the soft chime of calling birds,
and realize you never quite heard anything
before with such clarity.
You will come to know love in a way
you cannot presently begin to imagine.
It will fill your body and being
with such force and intensity
you will laugh and cry all at once,
then settle into a hushed state
of utter and complete peace.
You will finally know for certain
what One really means.
Grab tight to this light
and join me on the other side
where your pain is transformed
into the precise opposite fit of joy.

THE SPACE BETWEEN THE STARS
Davis Luther.

I felt you just now...
Thinking of me... longing for me...
Touching me in your mind...
Closing your eyes,
With palms flat to shoulders
In self-embrace,
Hoping, wishing, dreaming
Those arms would soon be mine.
And I see but blindly...
I touch but only with flesh...
Shielding well my heart...
Surrounding myself with hopeful silence,
Enthralled with private passion,
Approach... withdraw... yet only to...
Approach again... and finally withdraw in doubt,
And suffer this strange empty melancholy,
For you are the space between the stars,
The dust that dims the moon,
The light that lifts my day,
The breeze that buoys my soul,
The cloud that cools my brow,
The stream that stays my thirst,
The whispers in the wind,
The end of all my longing.

I feel you still…
Smiling at my image in your mind,
Approaching.... then withdrawing,
Balancing the cost of chancing,
Against the risk of losing,
And your heart skipped a beat,
As the picture became complete.

We are
the space
between the stars.

VERSATILE ANIMAL

Liselotte Holm.

You turn me into a versatile animal
With many layers
Of skins
Shining
Beneath
Invisible scars
Of scented letters.
Circle me
With your waving fins,
Those waving fins
Of your
Breath
Alone,
Those waving fins
In you.
My Scars
Are calling for your
Breath
Alone
To Heal
Open.
So Dive
Through
The rainbow
Of my irises
Into the depths
Of my eyes
And swim
Beneath
The animal
Of the me-word.
Swim
In the Ravenous Force
Beyond our control,
Circle me
In your Breath
Alone
Reinvent
Us.

Pried Open Heart

Shelley Haggard.

Hand captured:
digits gripped
and held over your heart.

I watch you sleep
with eyes questioning
and sharp.

You have pulled
the sword from
this stone of a heart.

Unfrozen, I can now
reach out for long lost love
in all it's glory.

I lament having wasted
so much time before beginning
this great love story.

Yet what has been wasted,
when I have been waiting
for someone such as you?

A hard case, I may have gone untouched,
but you have struck a cord in me
and I relinquish my all to you.

I TRAVEL YOUR LENGTH

Geraldine Green.

"I travel your length
like a river,
I travel your body
like a forest."

Fr. 'Piedra de Sol' Octavio Paz.

I travel your length as a wanderer would a desert,
searching for water to drink.

I find it in the soft contours of you,
the way tears are held

in slight folds of skin,
in the corner of your eyes,

the way colours run from an artist's palette,
the length of you in sunlight,

like a full moon
through a stained glass window.

I travel your body as a mariner would the sea,
first descending on your feet,

silently amazed at the thin veins spreading
wide into your broadening foot,

each line a single journey
of kisses and stroked flesh,

each fine veined fishing vessel,
each net a catch of quick-tongued licks.

I travel your body like an astronaut searching
for amazing moons of goodness.

I try to rise but am pulled down
each time by silk blowing,

a balloonist held captive
by the gravity of your body.

Eye Sense

Patricia Carragon.

We come together,
Play pantomime with eyelids,
Blink in slow motion.
Syncopation moves
On city streets
After rain decided to leave.

Spicy smells on a grill
Heat up aromatic conversation.
Love grows from sidewalk cracks
And takes off,
Like two pigeons
Flying toward Central Park
And their private alcove
By the lake.

We have cappuccino and pastries
At an outdoor café,
Watch a skyscraper rise
In the distance.
Eye sense sees more
Than friendship.
We turn away
And kiss.
We might as well reside
In the whipped cream clouds
On our sky-blue plates,
Since we do not see
That there are guests
Feasting on our crumbs.

STAR MOTHER AND THE AFRICAN TWINKIE TREE

Heather Moon Sofran.

"Which animal would be first?"
You ask me as we recline in bed.
Laughter bubbles in our throats
And sticks to the evening,
Like jungle condensation,
Like billions of galaxies unseen
In a half-empty cut-rock glass.

Your nonsense relieves me,
For Star Mother has refilled you,
Sprinkling you with her magic dust
When I wasn't looking.

As your body takes the shape
of Leo crouching in the night,
With comet-laced star dust seeds
Swelling in your loins,
You stalk me with wild savannas
Dancing green behind your eyes.

Submitting myself
To your cloudless night,
I present my latest confection to you,
Delightfully wrapped and frosted,
Like your twinkie tree in Africa,
And with billions of suns
Setting in the west behind me,
I wait for you to decide, in fact,
Which animal will be first.

To Him

Jillian Parker.

Who has read,
who has made
those inscriptions
in the soul of my skin
and on the slope of my shoulders?
That same scribe
sent me a scroll
sight unseen,
a spirit parchment.
How it flew and lodged
in the centre,
and I thought I was a woman,
or at least a giddy girl,
until I looked up and saw Him
and froze into a pillar,
an obelisk marked,
a map,
a chamber
of hidden treasure
in a walled city
awaiting
the author.

SOMETIMES LOVE COMES EASY

Carol Voccia.

I love the smile of your
Eyes that light up
As you express your most
Hidden secret of the day
In between the oohs and ahs
Of impossible
Situations that make us laugh
Because you will find the
Fun in all of it
Even when its not.

My heart sings as you look
At the wonderment of life in its
Absurdity and reach out
And embrace it anyway as
Warmly as you embrace me when
We hello or goodbye.

And I love you think family
Is your most prized possession
As you let the ins and outs of life's
Games take the course it will.
You steer the helm
But you know
The gods will have their way
With us anyway.

And I read between your lines
As you stutter in the fog of
Confusion,
Because the heart of you
Will be kind in the
Wake of the harsh you
Try to un-wrong.

And I love you because
You ask the universe for
Guidance and then hold me
Tight while waiting for the
Answers.

WINTERIZED

Michéle Vassal-Ring.

You are not defined by days in August
when night exacerbated, failed you
and light precipitated itself reckless
towards the melancholy of autumn, no more
than you are defined by the screaming greens
of April and the exuberance of peonies.
You, my love, are defined by December nights
that leak into mornings and the smell of fires
and roasted chestnuts, our love making as rich
and smooth as hot chocolate in Le Café de Flore,
and the warmth of notes you bend to ease me,
and the kindness of your hands, and the flour of your skin,
and the flannelette of your kisses blanketing me.
Us, again, winterized as in our beginning.

TRANSFORMING MOMENTS

Matthew Griffiths.

Many years of constant roaming,
Moving ever on alone,
Brought me to this distant dwelling,
Where at last I found my home.

Something subtle in her manner,
To transform nomadic heart,
Storm tossed waves becalmed by summer,
Winds of change at last depart.

Not the kiss, though so enticing,
Nor fine gifts given in love,
Can explain this rarest feeling,
Peace descending from above.

Being in her very presence
Strikes a chord within my soul,
At this joining, pure in essence,
Fractured spirits are made whole.

Heav'nly gift or fate decided?
Who can tell what brought us nigh?
Bonded by true love requited,
Tears replaced by lover's sigh.

EXPRESSIONS

Naome James.

I want to write you,
to speak you into words unspoken,
engrave the glades of your hollow
with the lexis of my centre.

I want to stroke you,
to finger the carvings of your sculpted soul,
recording to memory your marks
penned on the lost leaves of time.

I want to compose you,
to compile you into an anthology
of thoughts inscribed, tracing your path
that has led you to this place

of perpetuity.

HANDMADE IN
THE HEART

Catherine Rose.

I have woven a blanket,
stitched kisses of gold,
edged satin caresses
to cocoon you from cold.

I have harvested honey,
braved many spiked stings,
and bottled you nectar
the flower's heart brings.

I have built us a shelter
at the cusp of the storm;
the world cannot breach it.
You are safe, nourished, warm.

OLD GUITARS

Chuck Steffan.

She gave me
Closet space,
And resurrection
After my fall from grace,
This rusty wheel
Is still turning,
For every lost moment,
There is still a place,
Arrival, at last,
From a long departure.

And heart strings,
Like old guitars
Not played for years,
Long out of tune,
Just hanging on the wall,
Are dusted off
And tuned again.
They remember
Those melodies
That seemed forgotten.
Timeless songs
Of love's refrain,
Retrieved from
The remains
Of wistful ballads
From whence
they came.

Rainbows

Dianne Arthur.

And on the way home
from the Black Hills
you said I was perfect,

in the silence and the sun,
after the rain, the rain,
and the girl from Prussia Cove.

We were too tired to talk
after three sleepless nights
in fields full of strangers
talking, talking late into dark

layer on layer of music
drumming, parties
in the mud and the storms.

We lay under canvas,
so close; were we one or two?
It is no matter.

You imprinted onto my soul,
my funny man, chasing rainbows.

And we drove on through endless
counties, just you and me and the sun
and the clouds and the horizon,

and I never once told you that
rainbows were my downfall.

THE ARCHITECTURE
OF HAPPINESS

Joyce Åkesson.

Days filled
with hope and maturity.

Hours containing
our most happy moments:
a tender look,
a glass of wine,
a freshness,
a giddiness.

My spirit is charmed
by the moonlight stretched on the floor,
by the resonance of the truth,
by the aura surrounding your head.

We know how to share
our memories,
our dreams and hopes,
our personal talents,
the art of living,
the pleasure of giving,
the architecture of happiness.